Love

Peace

Light

by Indigo Fields

Introduction

This book is not a self help book as in "I will tell you to clean your spaces, drink water and sort your life out". It may be in the same house but a different room. This is the "stop, drop and roll" room. This is the ER. I will suggest how you may stop an emergency emotional state and how to reverse it. You may use this book as you wish. All I want is that you benefit from it.

The knowledge and suggestions in here are eclectically gathered from Daoism, traditional Chinese medicine and Eastern philosophy. None of this is my own or new.

I have refrained from the use of certain words because they're so overused it feels to me like they've lost their original meaning.

This book is kept as simple as possible to reach you more effectively.

Suggested use

Chapter One is the ER. The acute state. This is where we purge the negative emotions. Anger, anxiety or panic is dealt with here. We acknowledge, stop it and let it out. We also shut the door on it.

Chapter Two is where we, in lieu of better words, calm down. We clean the vessel and get a void space where the negative emotions now have left a hole. This is where we find and ground point zero.

Chapter Three is where we let the good stuff back in and welcome the positive emotions. We rise back up and with the good forces we stay up.

Each word is repeated 9 times with the exception of the countdown in the very first part of Chapter One. Breathe deeply, hold your breath if you like and say the word, or think it, on the exhale. Allow yourself to feel it all. Also allow yourself to let go. This is often the hardest part. Remember why you are doing this.

Go from chapter One to Three in one session or repeat where you get stuck or feel you're not done. In a tighter situation, use the countdown and then the following words once per page. Repeat as needed.

Use the notes spaces as you see fit. It's your book. Stick words, photos, memories or doodle there. Roll it up and hold it in your hand if you need to feel connected. This book was written by another human being, manufactured and delivered by others. We all breathe the same air. If you've got the ebook, write out the questions with your answers and keep them handy, take a picture and keep it on your phone or by your bed or fridge.

If your pain becomes too much, reach out to somebody. Call a hotline if you need to. Don't make final decisions when being upset.

We are connected. You are not alone.

/ Indigo

Chapter One

Purge the negative

One

Two

Three

Four

Five

Six

Seven

Eight

Nine

Out

Out

Out

Out

Out

Out

Out

Out

Out

NO

NO

NO

NO

NO

NO

NO

NO

NO

Chapter Two

Creating calm

Breathe

Breathe

Breathe

Breathe

Breathe

Breathe

Breathe

Breathe

Breathe

Settle

Settle

Settle

Settle

Settle

Settle

Settle

Settle

Settle

Let go

Let go

Let go

Let go

Let go

Let go

Let go

Let go

Let go

Chapter Three

Letting in positive

Calm

Calm

Calm

Calm

Calm

Calm

Calm

Calm

Calm

Light

Light

Light

Light

Light

Light

Light

Light

Light

Love

Love

Love

Love

Love

Love

Love

Love

Love

Notes

What do these meditation words
mean to me?

Is there one in particular that holds
a stronger power?

What works when I'm upset to soothe me?

What do I need to shut out from my life that only causes me pain?

Have I learned anything from holding on to it?

What do I truly fear?

What gives me genuine and lasting joy?

How can I make my joy the stronger of the two?

Last note from author:

Please;

Do not waste

Do not lay to waste

This includes yourself

www.ingramcontent.com/pod-product-compliance
Lightning Source LLC
Chambersburg PA
CBHW060821260726

48660CB00003B/1035